D0459663

LOOK HAMLET

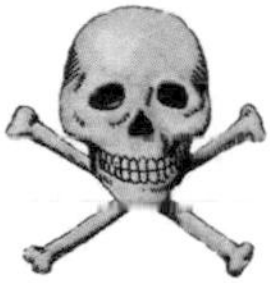

By Barbro Lindgren

Illustrations by Anna Höglund

Translated from the Swedish by Rachel Willson-Broyles

RESTLESS BOOKS
BROOKLYN, NEW YORK

Text copyright © Barbro Lindgren and Karneval förlag, Stockholm 2017
Illustration copyright © Anna Höglund and Karneval förlag, Stockholm 2017
Translation copyright © 2019 Rachel Willson-Broyles
English edition published in agreement with Koja Agency

First published as *Titta Hamlet*
by Karneval förlag, Stockholm, 2017

The cost of this translation was defrayed by a subsidy from
the Swedish Arts Council, gratefully acknowledged.

First Restless Books hardcover edition October 2019

Hardcover ISBN: 9781632062598
Library of Congress Control Number: 2019933973

Cover design by Jonathan Yamakami
Cover illustration by Anna Höglund

Printed in China

1 3 5 7 9 10 8 6 4 2

Restless Books, Inc.
232 3rd Street, Suite A101
Brooklyn, NY 11215

www.restlessbooks.org
publisher@restlessbooks.org

This book is published in memory of actors
Joan Sparks Baker (1932–2018)
and Abraham Stavans (1933–2019)

Look Hamlet.

Hamlet not happy.

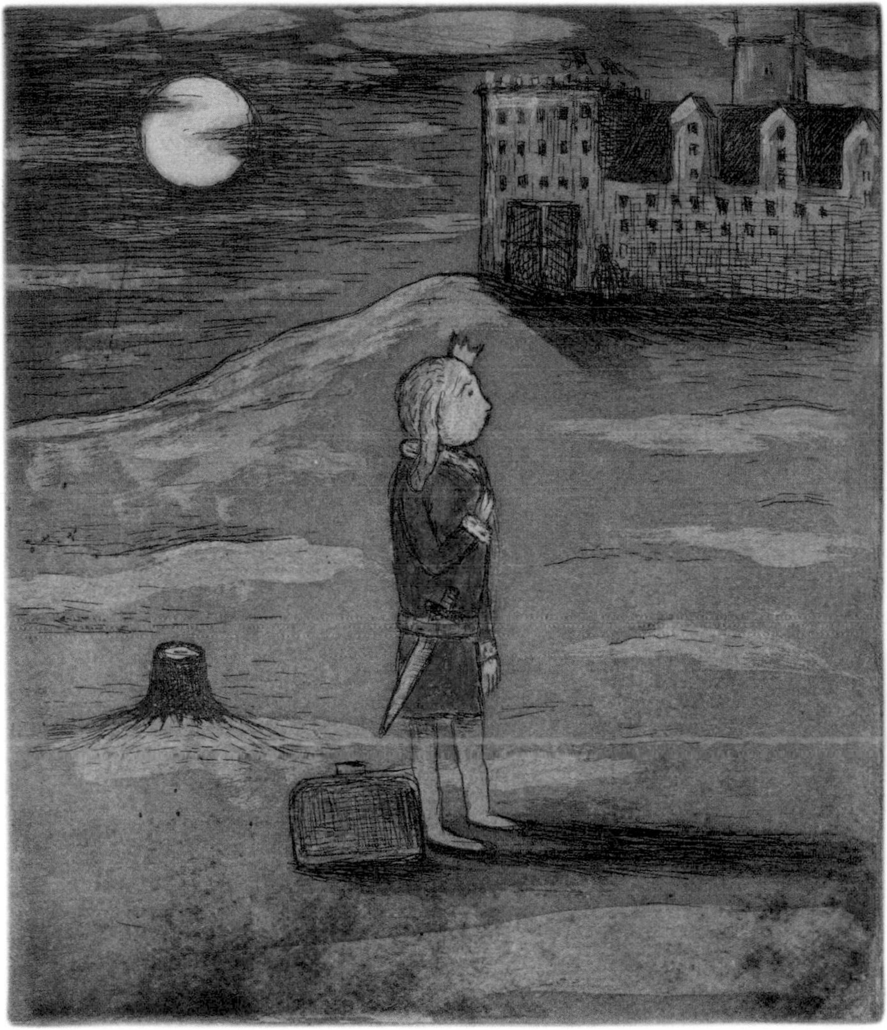

Hamlet's mommy dumb.
Hamlet's daddy dead.

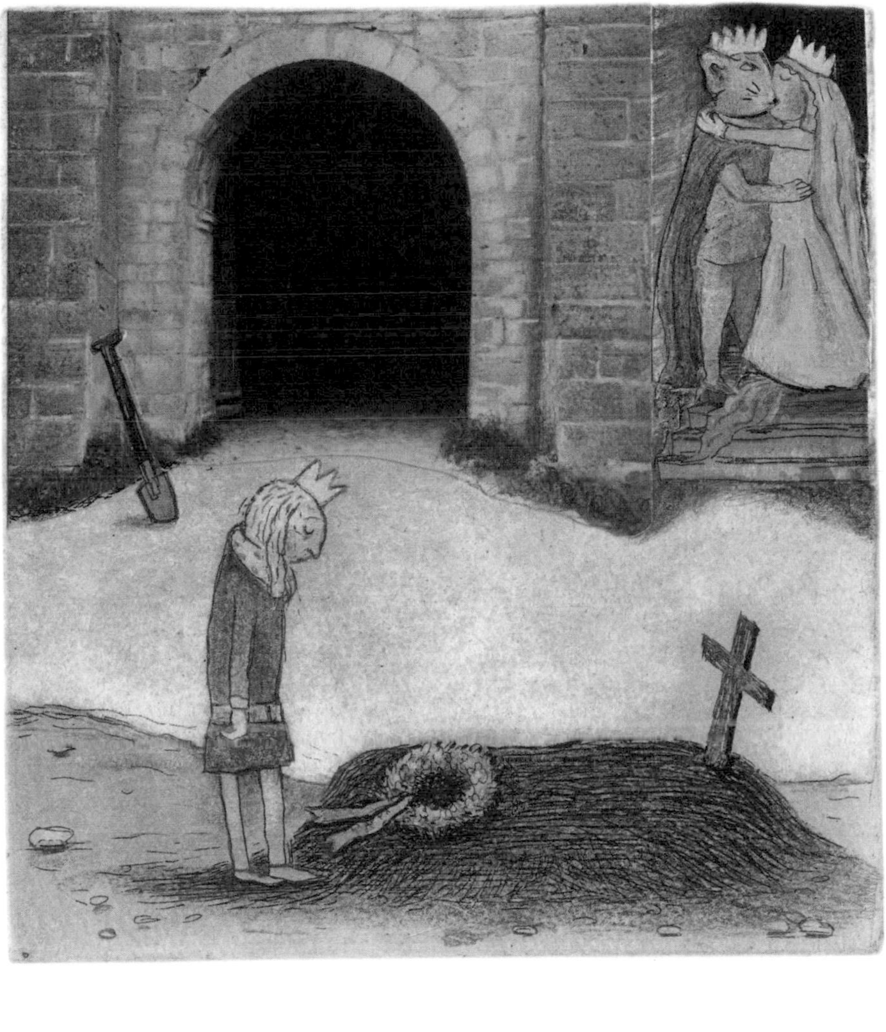

Hamlet gets other daddy.
Other daddy super dumb.

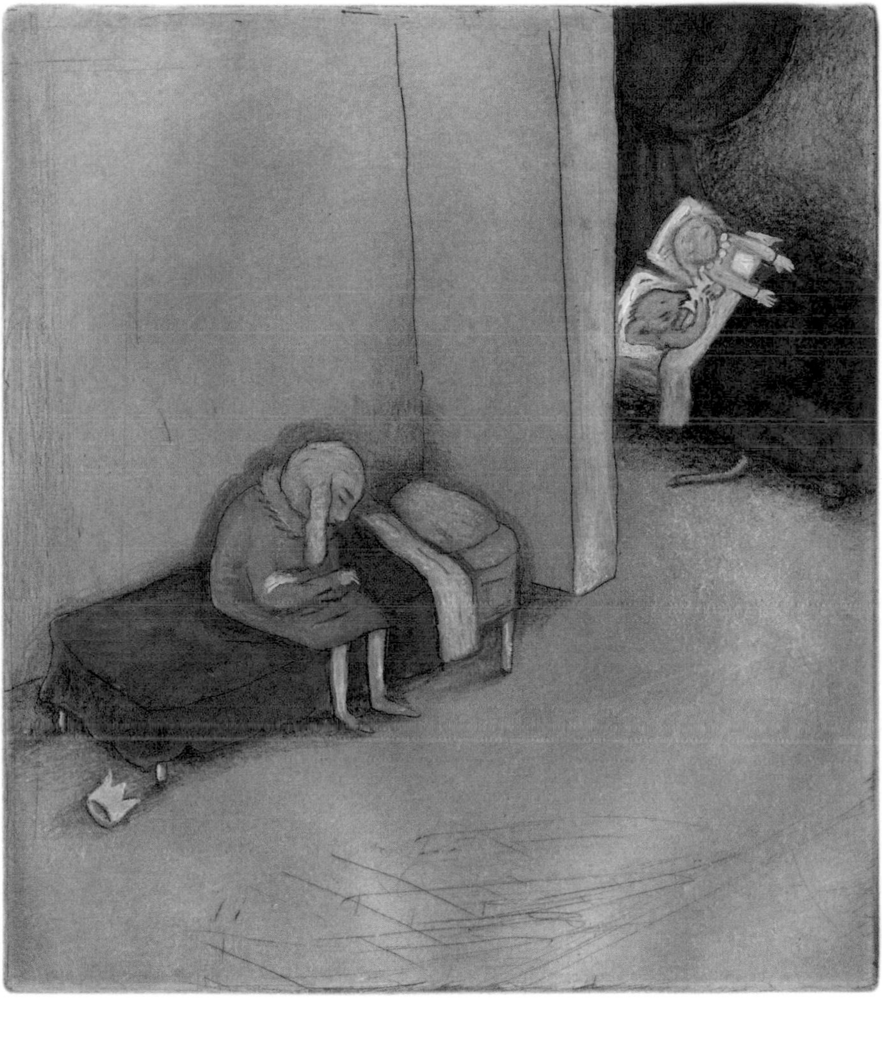

Hamlet's daddy ghost now.

Ghost can talk.

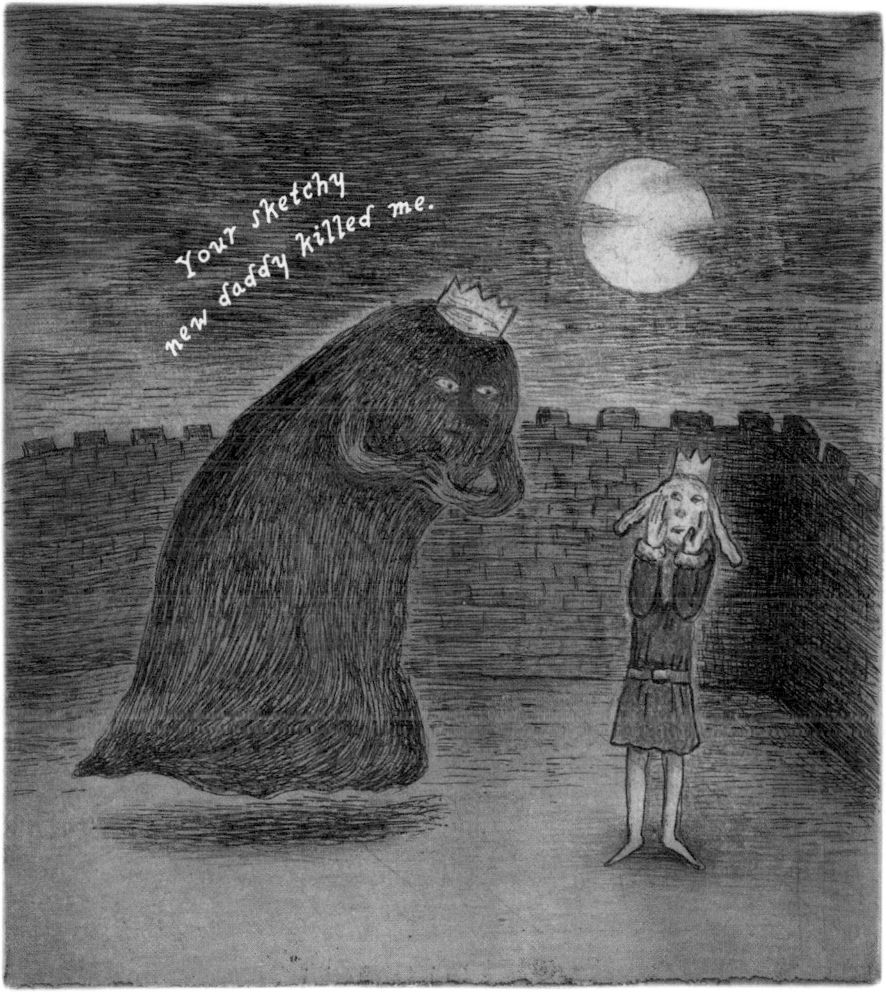
Your sketchy
new daddy killed me.

Hamlet hearts Ophelia.

Ophelia hearts Hamlet.

Ophelia's daddy sketchy.

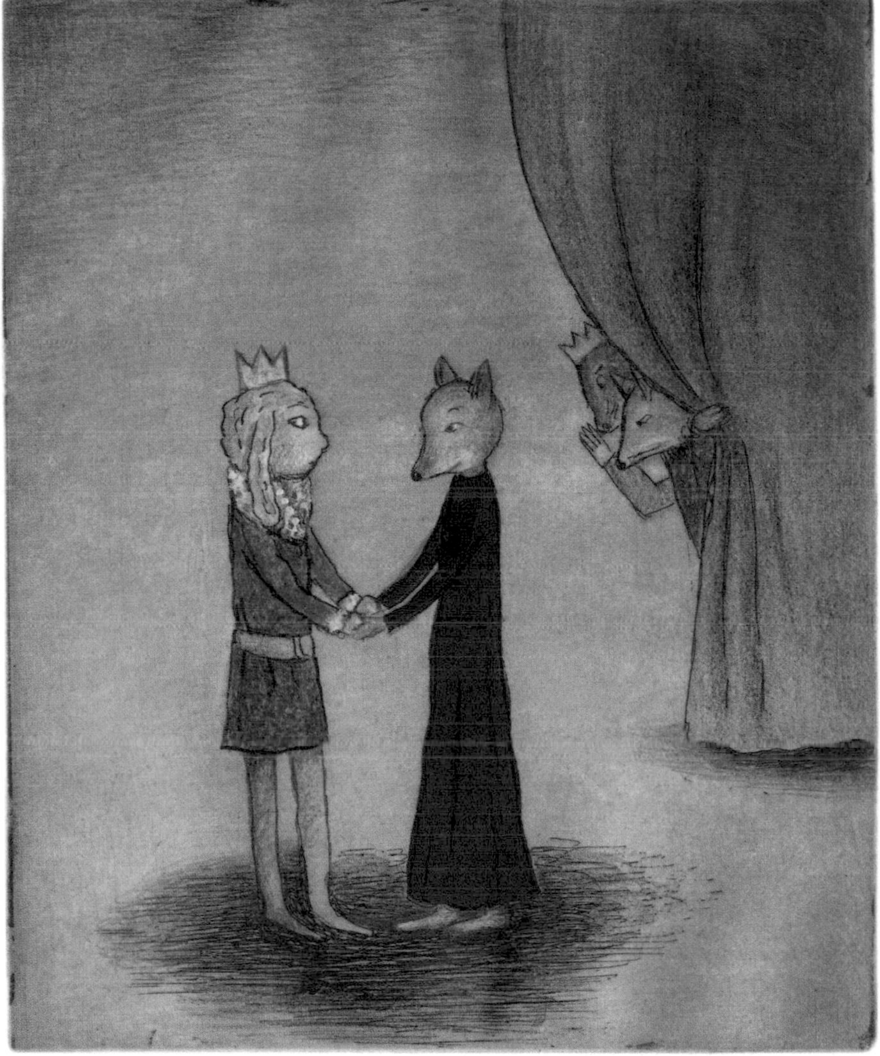

Hamlet crazy now.

Hamlet swords Ophelia's daddy.

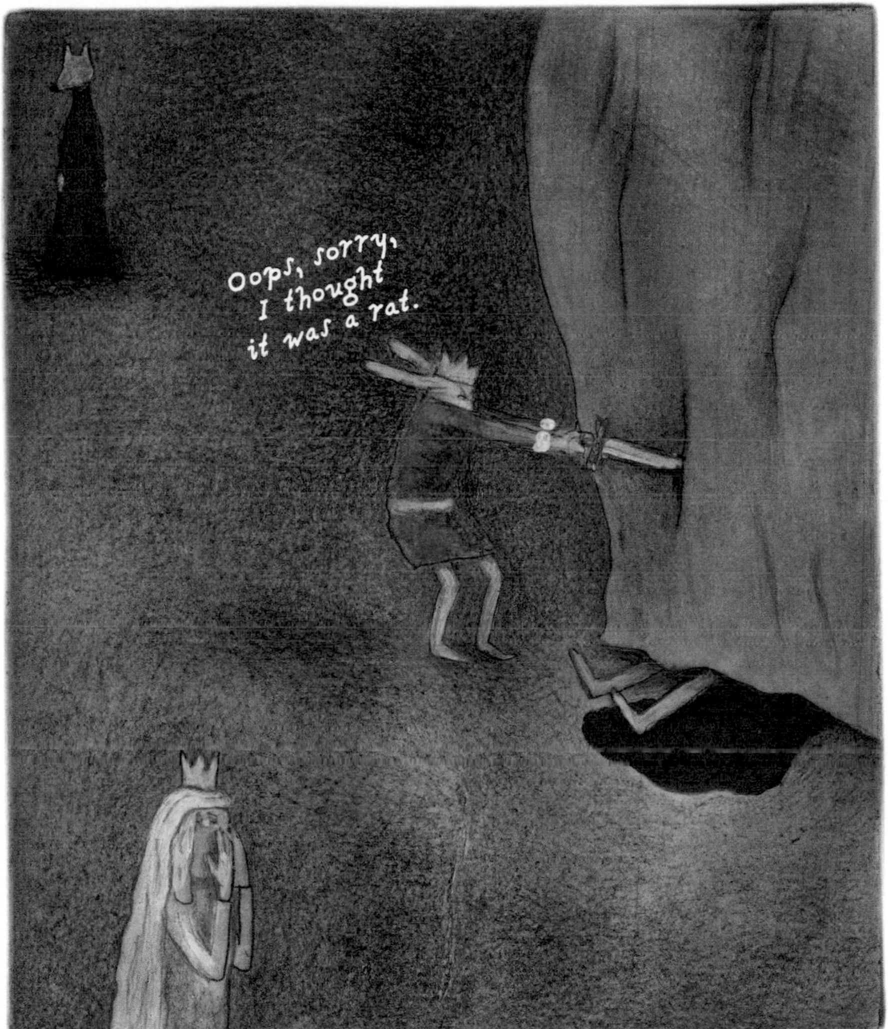
Oops, sorry, I thought it was a rat.

Ophelia crazy too.
Ophelia falls in river.
Now Ophelia dead.

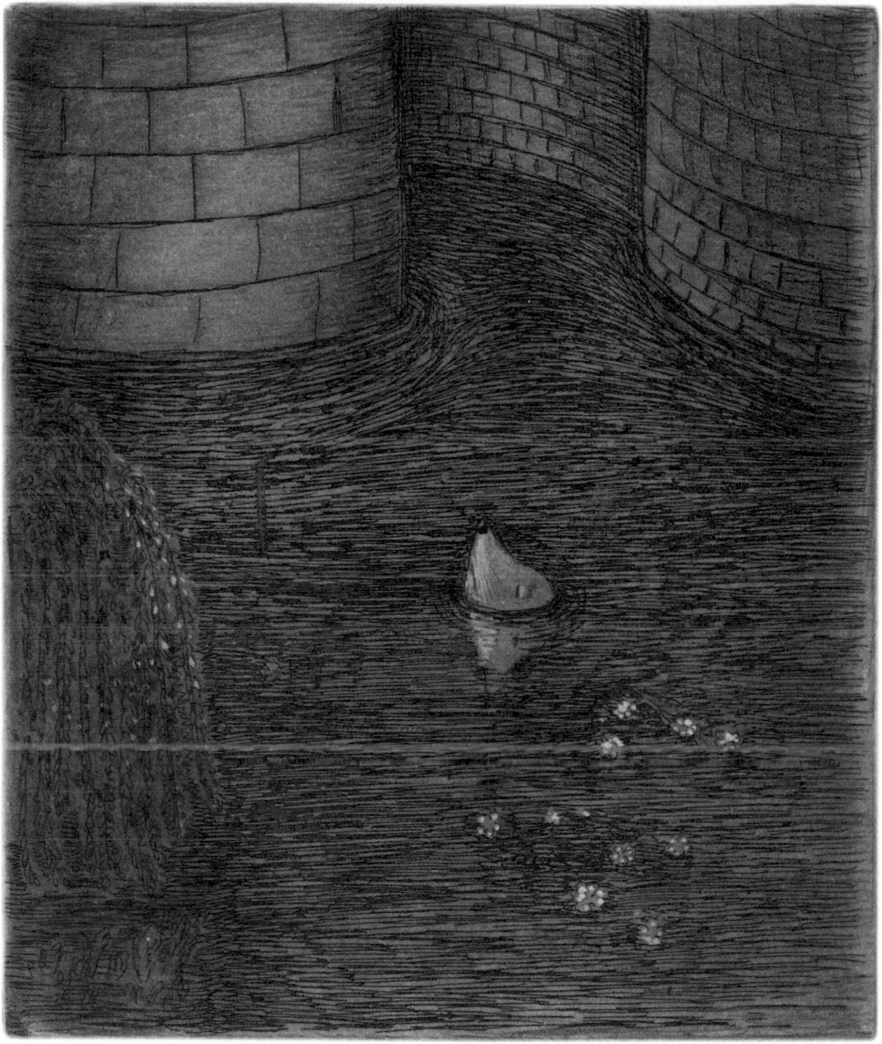

Hamlet super sad.

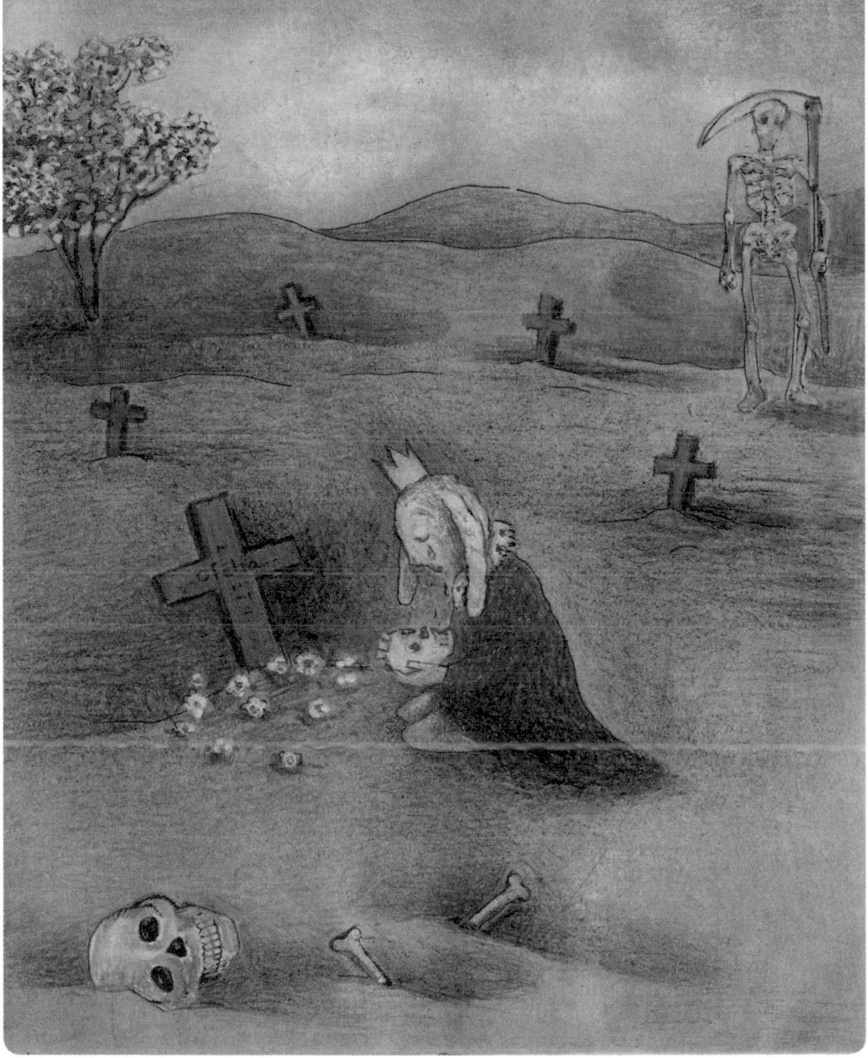

Sketchy daddy
wants to kill Hamlet.

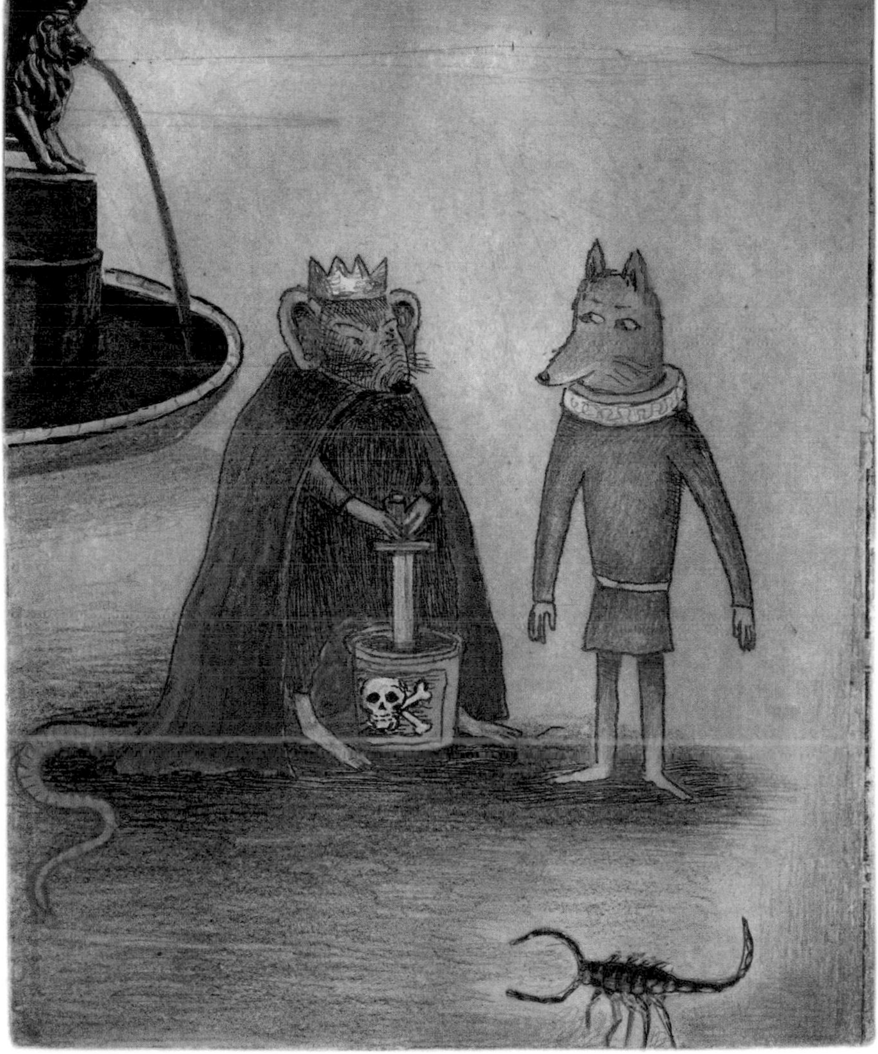

Ophelia's brother swords Hamlet.

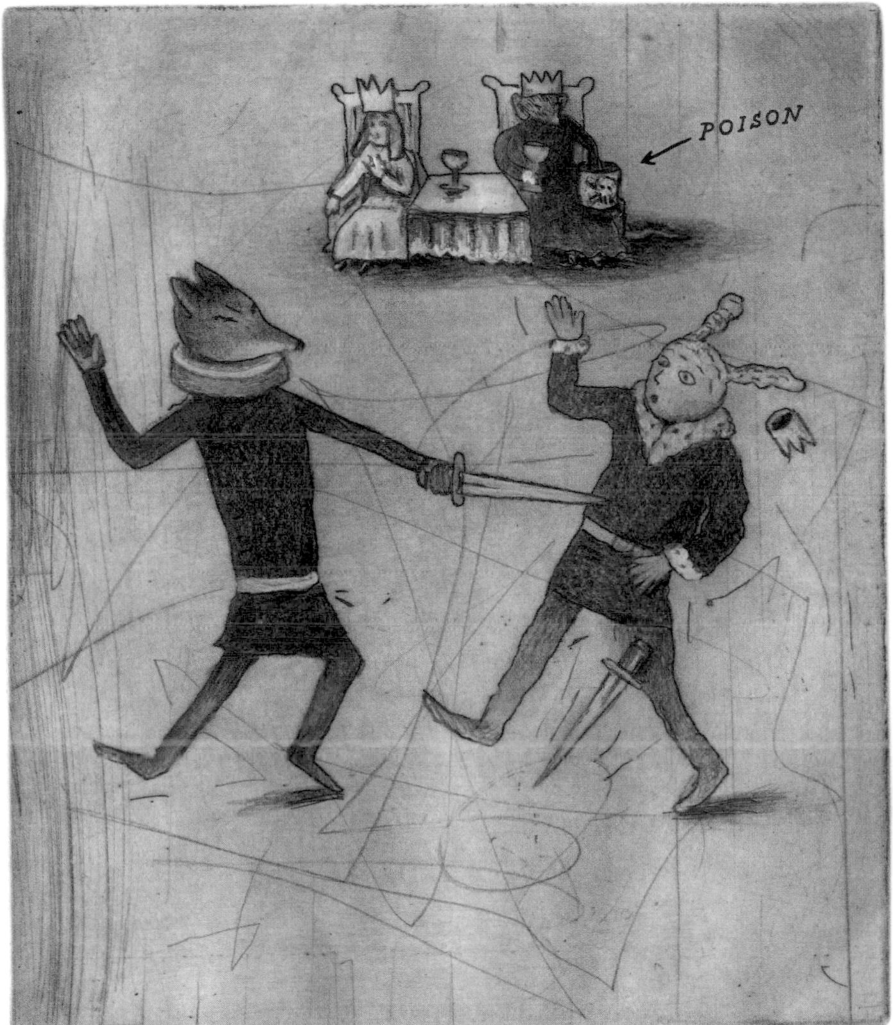
POISON

Hamlet swords Ophelia's brother.

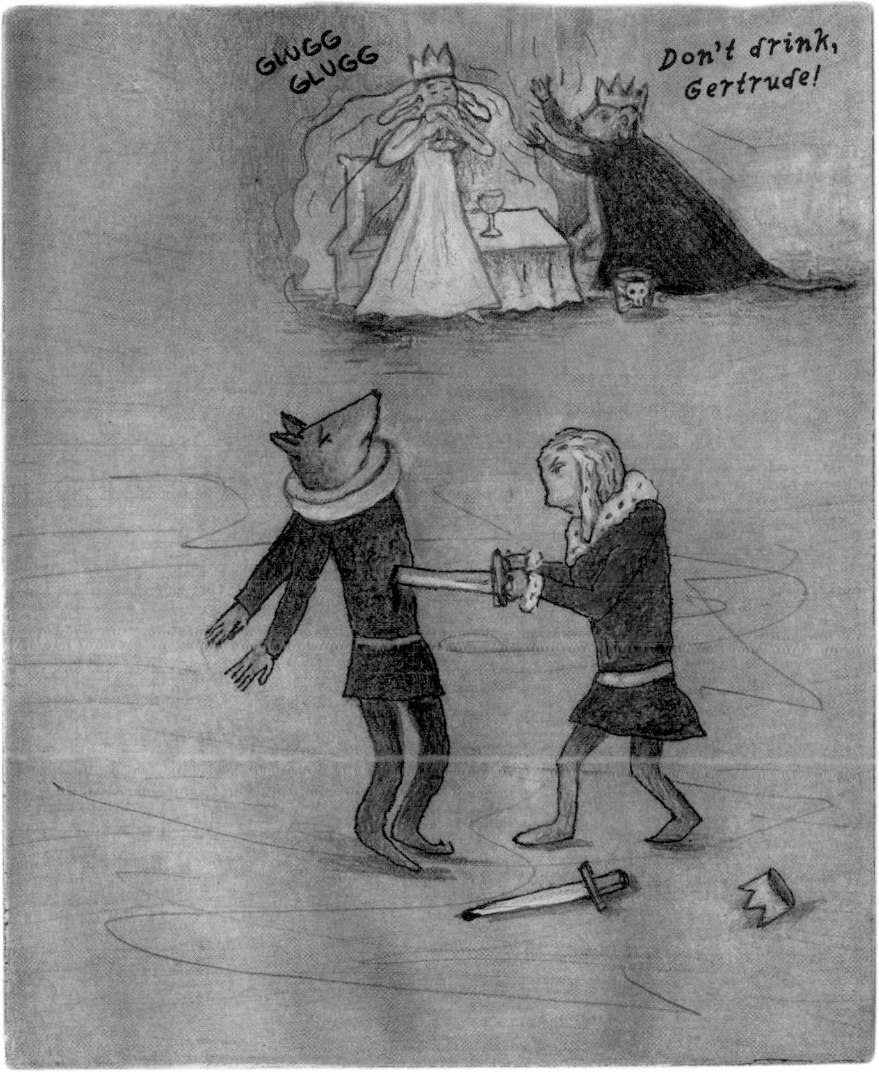
GLUGG
GLUGG
Don't drink,
Gertrude!

Hamlet's mommy drinks danger juice.
Now Hamlet's mommy dead.

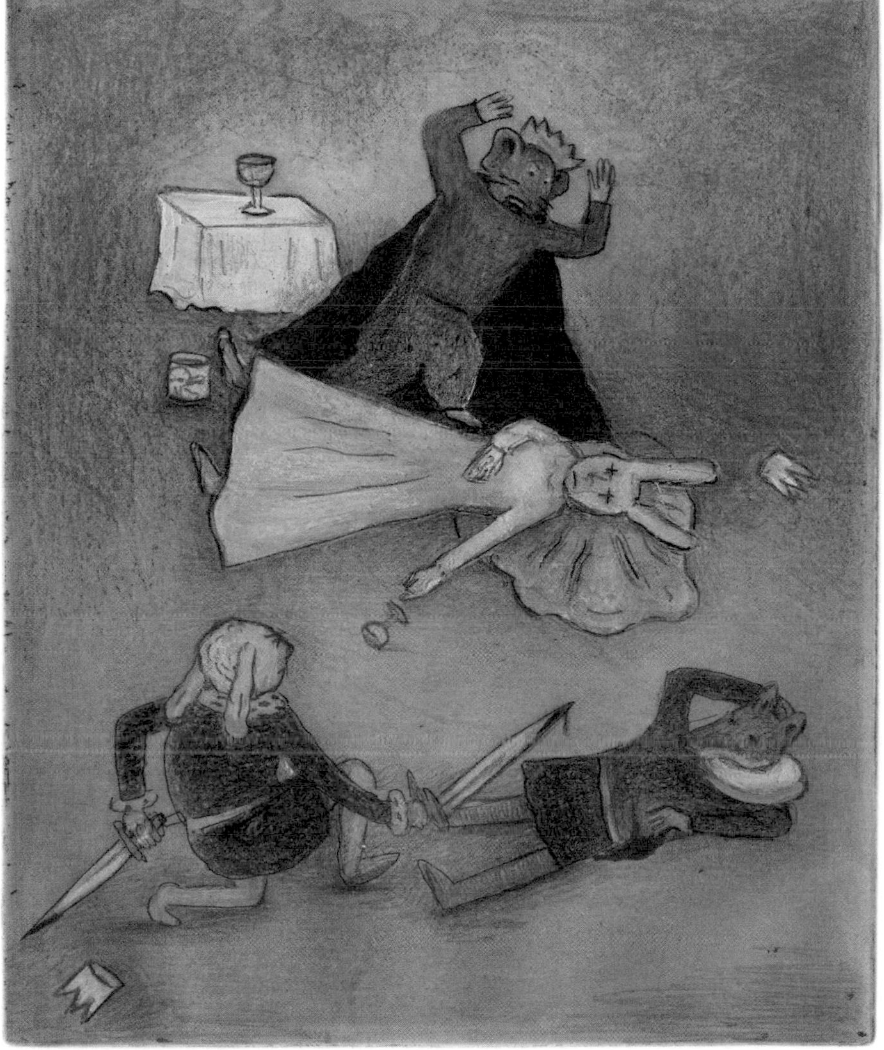

Hamlet swords sketchy daddy.
Now sketchy daddy dead.

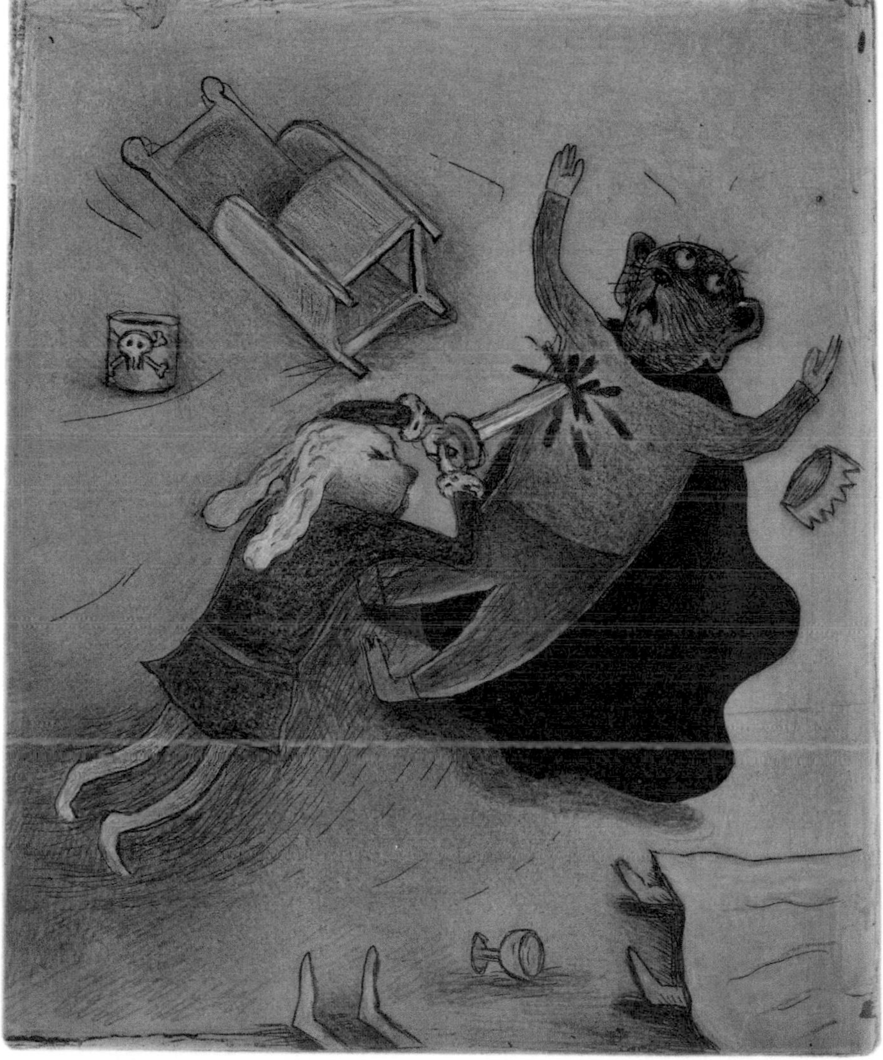

Ophelia's brother dead.

Hamlet dead.

Now everyone dead.

Nighty-night!

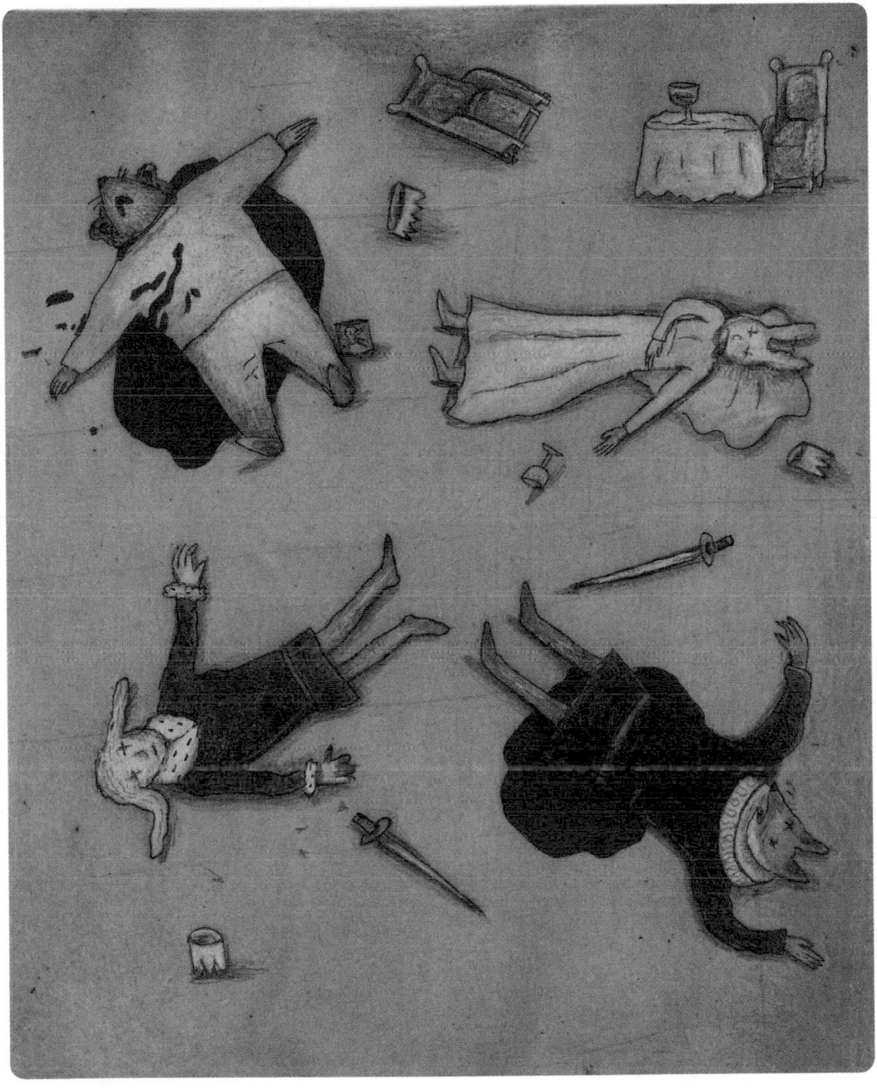

ABOUT THE AUTHOR:

Barbro Lindgren, born in 1937, is a Swedish author of innovative and multifaceted works for children of all ages. The winner of the world's largest children's literature prize, the Astrid Lindgren Memorial Award (ALMA), her body of work includes picture books, poetry, plays, and books for young adults. Since her debut as an author in 1965, she has published over a hundred titles, and her work has been translated into more than thirty languages.

ABOUT THE ILLUSTRATOR:

Starting out as a poor painter, artist **Anna Höglund** believed making picture books would put more solid food on the table for her family. It didn't really. But she discovered the possibilities of the medium, which today she still considers the ultimate: the crossbreeding of text and picture suits her perfectly. She has been doing this since 1982, when she was twenty-four.

ABOUT THE TRANSLATOR:

Rachel Willson-Broyles is a freelance translator based in Saint Paul, Minnesota. She received her BA from Gustavus Adolphus College and her Ph.D. from the University of Wisconsin-Madison. Her other translations include Jonas Hassen Khemiri's novels *Montecore* and *Everything I Don't Remember* and plays *INVASION!* and *I Call My Brothers*, Malin Persson Giolito's novel *Quicksand*, and Jonas Jonasson's novels *The Girl Who Saved the King of Sweden* and *The Accidental Further Adventures of the Hundred-Year-Old-Man*.

Restless Books is an independent, nonprofit publisher devoted to championing essential voices from around the world, whose stories speak to us across linguistic and cultural borders. We seek extraordinary international literature that feeds our restlessness: our hunger for new perspectives, passion for other cultures and languages, and eagerness to explore beyond the confines of the familiar. Our books— fiction, narrative nonfiction, journalism, memoirs, travel writing, and young people's literature—offer readers an expanded understanding of a changing world.

Learn more at restlessbooks.org.